EASTBOURNE
THEN and NOW

South Street grocer Cave Austin's delivery cart, *c*1913.

John Wilton

in association with

Chris Howden

S.B. Publications

By John Wilton:
Eastbourne, a Portrait in Old Picture Postcards, Volume 1, 1990 (with John Smith)
Eastbourne, a Second Portrait in Old Picture Postcards, Volume 2, 1991

This book is dedicated to Jeanne Holman

First published in 1999 by S. B. Publications
c/o 19 Grove Road, Seaford, Sussex BN25 1TP

ISBN 1 8570 176 3

Typeset by JEM Lewes
Printed and bound by The Adland Print Group Ltd
Unit 11, Bellingham Trading Estate
Franthorne Way
London SE6 3BX
Telephone 0181 695 6262

FOREWORD
by

**Sir Michael Richardson
Chairman of the Governors
St Andrew's School, Eastbourne.**

I am very happy to write the foreword to John Wilton's third volume of the pictures of old Eastbourne. When I was a boy at St Andrew's School in Meads in the 1930s, on Sunday the whole school went for a long, two to three hour walk, in the form of a crocodile.

We usually set out along the sea front and then walked back through the centre and east of Eastbourne, finishing up walking through Meads to the school. This gave all the children a great deal of time to look at the streets and architecture of the town, and whenever I drive to the school now it brings back memories of those happy times.

I am therefore delighted, having seen John Wilton's previous volumes, to support him in the production of this third volume which will be of great interest to all those who know the old Eastbourne, or who live in Eastbourne now and would like to see how it was in days past.

ACKNOWLEDGEMENTS

I am much indebted to Chris Howden who not only provided many postcards from his extensive collection, but took many of the present-day photographs. He has also helped me with additional research and acted as a runner, driver and friend. I am also most grateful to Kim Adam and Elizabeth Wilton for typing my manuscript. Many thanks, too, to the following people without whom this book would not have been possible:

For the loan of postcards and photographs: Phyllis Lewis, Anthony Thorpe, Steve Benz, Gill Kirkman of Eastbourne Borough Council, Mary Whiting and Hugh Wilton.

BIBLIOGRAPHY

A History of the Royal Eastbourne Golf Club, JJ Milton

A Short History of Eastbourne, L Stevens, 1987

Beachy Head, John Surtees, 1997

Black Diamonds and White Cliffs, J Hollands, 1982

Eastbourne, Pevensey, Seaford, Ward Lock & Co, 1914

Eastbourne, a Pictorial History, D Robert Elleray, 1978, 1995

Eight Town Walks, H Spears

Front Line Eastbourne, TR Beckett Ltd (Gazette and Herald) 1945

Guide to Eastbourne, R Armstrong, 1990

Guinness Book of Records, ed Norris McWhirter, 1984

Local Martello Towers, H Spears

Old Eastbourne, Rev W Budgen, 1912

Royal Visitors to Sussex, B Chapman, 1991

St Andrew's School 1877-1977, P Spillane, 1977

Sussex Place Names, Judith Glover, 1997

The Story of Eastbourne Lifeboats, J Morris and D Hendy, 1988

Wartime Eastbourne, G Humphrey, 1989

Eastbourne Gazette and Herald 1902-1999

The Daily Telegraph

The Times

pu = postally used

INTRODUCTION

The name Eastbourne means eastern stream, bourne being derived from the Old English word burna (stream). This stream rises near St Mary's Church in Old Town. In Saxon times a small settlement was established close to the stream. The Domesday Book records the village as Burne, and by the thirteenth century it was known as Estburn.

In the nineteenth century two great landowners, the Cavendish (Dukes of Devonshire) and the Gilbert families were responsible for the creation, planning and development of today's elegant town. The original master-plan was devised by the seventh Duke of Devonshire, his architect Henry Currey, George Ambrose Wallis (the Duke's agent and later the first mayor), and by Carew Davis Gilbert and his surveyor Nicholas Whitley.

A significant factor in the development of Eastbourne as a popular seaside resort was the construction of the London, Brighton and South Coast Railway, with the first locomotive arriving at Eastbourne Station in 1849. By 1870 the population had doubled and Eastbourne became known as the Empress of Watering Places as a result of its excellent climate and the patronage of the aristocracy.

During the Second World War Eastbourne was seriously damaged by enemy bombs and many fine buildings, including St John's Church in Meads, St Anne's Church, Upperton Gardens, and the Technical Institute and Free Library were destroyed.

In more recent years a large section of the cliff at Beachy Head crashed into the sea in what may well be Britain's biggest single loss of coastline in living memory. Just a short distance away the Belle Tout lighthouse was jacked up and moved 50ft inland to prevent it from falling into the sea, and on The Crumbles, to the east of the town, a massive harbour has been built and there are plans for a total of 3,500 houses. Yet, despite all the changes, the town has retained much of its charm and elegance.

John Wilton

BELLE TOUTE LIGHTHOUSE, EASTBOURNE.

THEN – BELLE TOUT LIGHTHOUSE *c*1920: Belle Tout, a 47ft high circular stone tower instigated by John Fuller MP, was first lit on October 11, 1834, but shortly afterwards it became obvious that the site was ill chosen. In theory the light was visible for miles, in practice it was often obscured by sea mist. As a result, the light remained in operation only until 1902, when it was replaced by the new Beachy Head lighthouse below the cliff. Belle Tout then became a private residence. During the Second World War it was used as a target during gunnery practice and by 1944 the building was a wreck. In the 1950s Dr Edward Revill Cullinan leased Belle Tout and started rebuilding in August 1956. His widow sold the lease a few years later

NOW: On October 18, 1967, a tenant hanged himself from the staircase. In 1986 the lighthouse and surrounds were upgraded by BBC TV to use for three weeks' film location work, in the series *The Life and Loves of a She-Devil.* The chalk cliffs are constantly eroding, and in March 1999 the Grade II listed building was moved 50ft back from the cliff edge. Engineers dug down six feet and put in place specially-designed steelwork and hydraulic stools to ease the building back from the edge.

THEN – BEACHY HEAD LIGHTHOUSE: In 1902 Trinity House replaced Belle Tout with a new lighthouse at the base of Beachy Head. It was constructed of 720 Cornish granite blocks conveyed from the railway station by a traction engine. The lighthouse is 142ft high, 50ft in diameter at the base and has eight rooms. It is a quarter of a mile from the cliffs, and its light can be seen forty miles out to sea. The lighthouse was manned throughout the Second World War, but although the cliffs behind were hit on many occasions it escaped unscathed.

NOW: The two pictures look very similar, but this is deceptive. The soft chalk cliffs are eroding at an alarming rate. In January 1999 a section of the cliff crashed into the sea in what may be Britain's biggest single loss of coastline in living memory. The chalk almost reached the lighthouse after thousands of tonnes fell 500ft into the sea. In 1983 the working of the lighthouse was automated and the keepers withdrawn. The lighthouse featured on the 22p postage stamp for the Safety at Sea issue on June 18, 1985.

38102. BEACHY HEAD HOTEL, EASTBOURNE.

THEN – BEACHY HEAD HOTEL, *c***1950:** The hotel, formerly known as the Queen's Hotel, was destroyed by fire, first in the 1920s, and a second time on April 6, 1966. The rebuilt hotel was taken over by brewery giant Whitbread and re-opened in the spring of 1994 following a £650,000 refit, which included an enlarged Beachy Head Countryside Centre.

NOW: On December 10, 1994 the hotel was burned to the ground again. Without delay Whitbread built an enlarged Brewer's Fayre restaurant and bar to re-open the following summer. Included was Eastbourne Borough Council's Beachy Head Countryside Centre, where there is an exhibition of the history and ecology of Beachy Head and Eastbourne's Downland.

Meads Eastbourne.

E. Cole, Meads Library Eastbourne.

THEN – MEADS FROM ABOVE UPPER DUKE'S DRIVE: This rare card, sent in July 1905, shows, in the foreground, houses at the lower end of Rowsley and Edensor Roads. On the far side of Wellcombe Crescent is St Andrew's School, founded 1877. Darley Road joins Wellcombe Crescent from the left, with Aldro School, founded 1897 by the Rev Harold Browne, brother of the Rev Edwin Browne, headmaster of St Andrew's School 1890-1933, just below the junction. Aldro was evacuated to Shackleford near Godalming at the outbreak of the Second World War, and there it still flourishes. On August 16, 1940 a Messerschmitt ME110 crashed in the grounds of Aldro. The dead pilot fell onto the roof of Hill Brow Prep School and the rear-gunner drowned when he parachuted into the sea.

NOW: The photograph is taken from the same angle, but from lower down. This is because the slopes on the Downs are now heavily wooded. St Andrew's School and its playing fields are still visible. The Aldro site is now part of the University of Brighton and most of the trees visible in the centre of the postcard have been cut down and replaced by modern housing.

Eastbourne from Beachy Head

THEN – VIEW FROM THE FOOT OF BEACHY HEAD, pu1909: Behind the private house in the foreground stood St Luke's Children's Hospital, opened by the Prince of Wales in 1891 while he was staying at Compton Place with Princess Alexandra. Further back and to the left is All Saints' Hospital. On July 19, 1869, the completed building was blessed and declared open by Samuel Wilberforce, Lord Bishop of Winchester.

NOW: The view is similar today, although two new buildings have appeared recently. St Luke's Children's Hospital has been replaced by Dolphin Court, a block of flats opened in 1965 and the 19-storey South Cliff Tower dominates the skyline. Film buffs may be interested to know that the white cliffs visible in the film *The Battle of Britain* are those of Beachy Head and the Seven Sisters, not Dover, and that South Cliff Tower, although not completed until 1966, features in this film set in 1940.

HOLY WELL, RETREAT, EASTBOURNE

THEN – HOLYWELL RETREAT, pu1914: Gore Chalk Pit was laid out as gardens in 1905 at a cost of £400. In 1922 it was converted into Holywell Italian Gardens. Even in the driest of summers water trickles out from the base of the cliffs. The name Holy Well is believed to originate from the 14th century as a spring below an ancient burial mound on the cliffs.

NOW: Near the end of the promenade, just visible on the extreme left, are chalets let annually by the Eastbourne Borough Council. Chalet 2 was used in March 1935 by King George V and Queen Mary when they stayed in Eastbourne. Also visible is one of the Dotto trains which now convey holiday makers along the promenade. On the beach large quantities of shingle from the Isle of Wight are being used to recharge the area as part of the coastal protection scheme.

THEN – THE WESTERN LAWNS, *c*1908: At the turn of the century large numbers of the 'well-to-do' would take a leisurely Sunday morning stroll on the Western Lawns. Dressed in their finery, they demonstrated their position in society and also, perhaps, the fact that they had been to Morning Service and had a cook at home to prepare luncheon. In his book *Grand Hotel*, Peter Pugh wrote: 'Western Lawns on Sunday morning – this was the place to find a wife or husband'.

18

NOW: This photograph shows that dress code has changed considerably. Here RAF parachutists taking part in Eastbourne's annual air show arrive on the Western Lawns where the statue of the eighth Duke of Devonshire now stands. This statue was unveiled on Monday, October 24, 1910, by the Duke of Norfolk. The Wish Tower can still be seen and to its right are the Wish Tower Café and Sun Lounge.

Wilmington Gardens, Eastbourne

THEN – WILMINGTON GARDENS, pu1909: It is believed that the gardens were shared by residents of the buildings on either side of the square, and were divided into lots by hedges, there being no other gardens attached to the houses. In 1949 the gardens were 'gifted' to Eastbourne Borough Council by the Chatsworth Estate with a proviso that they should be properly maintained at all times.

NOW: At the far end of the square is the Congress Theatre, which was opened in 1963 and was recently awarded a Grade II listing for its special 1960s architecture. The building, which has made the town competitive as a conference centre, was designed by Bryan and Norman Westwood and Partners, and cost about £400,000. The buildings on the left remain, but on the right blocks of flats have replaced former hotels and flats.

LAUNCHING THE LIFEBOAT, EASTBOURNE

THEN – LAUNCHING THE LIFEBOAT: This 1910 postcard shows the *Olive* being hauled out of the William Terriss Memorial Boathouse, now the Eastbourne Lifeboat Museum. When in 1898 the RNLI decided to provide the town with a new lifeboat and boathouse, funds to pay for the boathouse were raised by the *Daily Telegraph* to commemorate the actor William Terriss who was assassinated outside the stage door of the Adelphi Theatre in London in 1897. The *Olive*, a 36ft Liverpool class boat, was built at a cost of £839, and paid for from a legacy of the Misses Wingate of Edinburgh.

NOW: In March 1937 Sir Godfrey Baring, chairman of the RNLI, opened the Terriss Boathouse as the first lifeboat museum in the UK. Here there are many photographs, including some of epic rescues, various items of lifeboat memorabilia and a fine selection of lifeboat models. Behind the museum can be seen, from the left, the Grand Court flats, which replaced the old Kenilworth and Mostyn Hotel, the Oban Hotel, which replaced private homes and boarding houses, and the Alexandra Hotel.

Alexandra Hotel, Grand Parade, East Bourne, Tel. 132

THEN – THE ALEXANDRA HOTEL AND THE DEVONSHIRE BATHS, pu1932: Carlisle Road separates the hotel from the Devonshire Baths, on the right. The baths, designed in 1872 by GA Wallis, the Duke of Devonshire's agent, and first mayor of Eastbourne, were opened on April 1, 1874, and contained two heated sea-water baths filled through an iron pipe from the beach below the Wish Tower. The larger bath was reserved for men, and the smaller one for women. Family bathing was allowed on Mondays, Wednesdays and Saturdays.

NOW: The exterior of the Alexandra has hardly changed in the last hundred years. The restaurant is still on the extreme right. The baths closed during the 1960s and the building's distinctive tower was demolished. Two new blocks of flats were due to be built on this site during 1999.

THEN – GRAND PARADE FROM THE WISH TOWER SLOPES, *c*1905: It was along here in 1848 that James Berry, the Earl of Burlington's surveyor, began to construct a sea wall made of green-sand from a nearby quarry. Bathing machines, which were horse-drawn, can be seen on the right of the picture. The bandstand, known as the Bird Cage, was built in 1893 at a cost of £300. It stood on cast iron stilts adjacent to the Lower Parade.

NOW: The new Grand Parade Bandstand was opened on August 5, 1935. The profile of the beach was changed recently by the building of new groynes and the pumping of half a million tonnes of shingle on to the shore to slow down the wash of shingle eastwards. The Mayfair Hotel, on the extreme left in the postcard, has been replaced by the £3+ million Transport and General Workers' Union Holiday and Conference Centre, opened on September 9, 1976, by Jack Jones.

21 · EASTBOURNE. — *The Parade.* — LL.

THEN – GRAND PARADE, pu1906: A horse omnibus, cabs and bath chairs provide the transport in this scene looking towards the Carpet Gardens, the Queen's Hotel and the pier. On the left is the Mayfair Hotel. The sign on the lamp post on the right shows the way down Lascelles Terrace to Devonshire Park. The Bird Cage bandstand can be seen further right.

NOW: Here, the horse-drawn vehicles have been replaced by buses, cars and taxis. The TGWU Centre has replaced the Mayfair Hotel. On the wall of the promenade facing the Grand Parade Bandstand, which replaced the Bird Cage, is a memorial plaque to John Wesley Woodward, a cellist in the Grand Hotel Orchestra, and one of the musicians who went down with the *Titanic* in 1912.

Lawn Tennis Tournament, Devonshire Park, Eastbourne.

THEN – TENNIS AT THE DEVONSHIRE PARK: The first South of England Grass Court Tennis Championships were held here in 1881. This 1905 card shows a ladies' double match in progress. Reggie Doherty, also featured on the card, was the elder of the famous brothers who dominated tennis between 1897 and 1907. He won the men's singles at Wimbledon four times and, with his brother Laurie, the doubles eight times. He died in 1910 aged thirty-six. Laurie won Wimbledon five times and was the only foreign winner of the US Championship in the first forty-five years of the event.

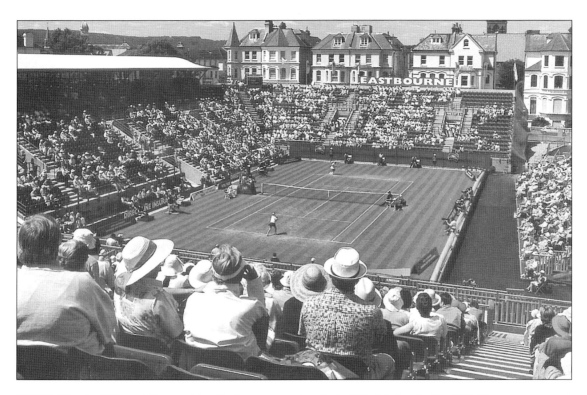

NOW: The facilities at Devonshire Park are second only to Wimbledon in the UK. Three permanent stands flank the centre court and a temporary stand is erected for major tournaments. Eastbourne plays host to the International Ladies Tennis Championships in June, LTA County Cup Tennis in July and the Legends' Series in July and August.

Entrance to Devonshire Park, Eastbourne. 608.

THEN – ENTRANCE TO DEVONSHIRE PARK, pu1908: This, the main entrance, led to the spacious iron and glass Floral Hall where concerts were given daily in the season. From October to June the hall was arranged as a Winter Garden. Above the Floral Hall is the Pavilion, used as a winter concert hall and ballroom. Here, said a 1914 guide book, 'cinematography and other entertainments are held'. The Floral Hall became the venue for important functions in the town, as well as providing for roller-skating and dancing.

NOW: Much has changed. Most of the glass in the roof has been replaced, initially by zinc panels and more recently by a material called Nuralite, and the hall is therefore much darker. No longer do palm trees and other exotic plants grow inside the building. The Devonshire Park is, however, an important part of Eastbourne's conference centre. The Winter Garden, a Grade II listed building, plays host to conference dinners, dances, exhibitions and tea dances.

1774 Eastbourne The Theatre Devonshire Park

THEN – THE DEVONSHIRE PARK THEATRE, pu1913: The theatre was designed by Henry Currey and opened in 1884. The entrance is flanked by two handsome Italianate towers which house the fireproof emergency staircases. In 1903 much of the interior was remodelled by Frank Matcham.

NOW: Full of quirky charm, the theatre is now a Grade II listed building. Special features include a royal loo built especially for Queen Victoria, and a cosy theatre bar. For those not wishing to avail themselves of strong drink, coffee or tea is served on trays in the interval.

THEN – THE LOWER PARADE AND PIER: In this 1907 postcard of the scene on the Grand Parade there were long dresses and hats for the women even on a scorching summer day, and they carried parasols to protect their complexions. For the men there were suits or blazers and flannels as well as hats and waistcoats. Notice the bathing machines at the water's edge.

NOW: The bathing machines have been replaced by bathing cabins. A red and yellow flag flies above the lifeguard's tower on the left of this photograph and the Bird Cage bandstand has gone, replaced by its more modern counterpart.

The Three Parades, Eastbourne.

THEN – THE THREE PARADES AND WISH TOWER, pu1909: In 1804 fixed defences against a possible Napoleonic invasion were established between Dover and Seaford in the form of small, circular fortifications called Martello towers (from a similar tower at Cape Mortella in Corsica). The Wish Tower, Martello Tower No 73, was manned by one officer and twenty-four men, with a heavy cannon mounted on top. In 1883 the tower was leased from the War Office by the town and became the home of the Hollobon family, who ran it as a small geological museum. During the Second World War the tower was equipped with six inch guns and became part of the south coast defences.

NOW: In 1959 the Wish Tower was given Ancient Monument status and the following year it was restored, and a 'sun lounge' was built nearby. In 1970 the tower opened as a museum and is now the home of the Puppet Museum, which exhibits puppets from all over the world, from television and the film world.

Eastbourne.   Off for a Sail.

THEN – ANY MORE FOR THE SKYLARK?: The 1897 edition of the town guide, called *Empress of Watering Places*, mentioned the numerous boats thronging the beaches and added: 'Without exaggeration, too, it may be stated that the fishermen of Eastbourne are of a superior class, being very civil and obliging, and rowdyism, such as is associated with many seaside boatmen, is unknown'. This postcard from 1908 shows holidaymakers off for a sail in the *Skylark*.

NOW: Allchorn's pleasure boats have been sailing for more than 130 years. They operate, weather permitting, from May until October. There are forty-five minute trips to Beachy Head and back, and hour and a half circular cruises taking in Beachy Head lighthouse, Birling Gap, the Seven Sisters, the Crumbles, the fishing and lifeboat stations and the Redoubt in July and August.

THE ROYAL SOVEREIGN LIGHTSHIP
EASTBOURNE.

THEN – THE ROYAL SOVEREIGN LIGHTSHIP, *c*1910: As the English Channel narrows into the Straits of Dover, many hidden shoals and sandbanks lie off the Sussex and Kent coast, causing serious hazards to shipping. In 1875 Trinity House established the *Royal Sovereign* lightship to mark the Royal Sovereign Shoal, seven miles off Eastbourne. Large vessels were required to keep a course to the south of the lightship.

NOW: In 1966 Sir William Halcrow and Partners was commissioned by Trinity House to investigate the feasibility of a light tower structure with a steel tower. The base and tower were constructed near Newhaven commencing in 1967 and finally positioned, after many delays, in 1971. The new light tower was 159ft high with the light visible for twenty-eight miles. The final cost was £1.7 million, almost double the estimate. In August 1994, at a cost of £180,000, the light tower was automated and the light range reduced to twelve miles.

Burlington Hotel and Flower. *Eastbourne.*

THEN – THE BURLINGTON HOTEL AND EASTBOURNE CARPET GARDENS: This postcard, written in French, and sent to an address in Belgium in 1899, is an example of a 'court card'. The first UK postcards bearing pictures were published in 1894. Early picture postcards were smaller in size than standard cards today, and the picture shared the space on one side with the correspondence. In 1902 the standard size was introduced and new Post Office regulations permitted one side to be used for the illustration and the reverse for the correspondence and address.

NOW: The Carpet Gardens have been in existence for well over one hundred years, and were originally referred to as 'flowering beds'. Thousands of plants are used every year on a seasonal basis, being, at times, thematic. Recently a lighthouse and a horse and cart were formed out of hedging plants etc. The gardens are cared for by Eastbourne Borough Council's parks and gardens department.

The "Brighton Queen" off Eastbourne.

THEN – *BRIGHTON QUEEN* LEAVING EASTBOURNE PIER, pu1912: Pleasure steamers sailed to the Royal Sovereign lightship, Brighton, Hastings and as far as Shanklin on the Isle of Wight. The paddle steamer *Brighton Queen*, built in 1897, was 240ft long and had a maximum speed of 20 knots. She made many cross-Channel excursions before being requisitioned by the Admiralty in 1914. On October 5, 1915, during mine-sweeping duties off Belgium, she struck a mine and sank.

NOW: MV *Balmoral* was launched in Southampton on June 27, 1949. She is 203ft 6in long, has a grt of 736 and a speed of 14.5 knots. She has operated mainly in western coastal waters, but since Eastbourne Pier was strengthened and restored in 1991 she has made regular visits to the town during the summer months. *Balmoral* is operated by the Waverley Steam and Navigation Company, and she is used on a variety of cruises, including a twelve-hour voyage along the coast to Kent, into the Thames estuary and up river to London.

Going the pace at **EASTBOURNE**

1608 C

GAY SPARK

THEN – SPEEDBOAT TRIPS: This card, sent in 1932, was probably printed in large numbers and overprinted to order with the name of any seaside town as required. Under the flap are twelve local views. The sender of the card, Frank, wrote on the back: 'In spite of the trade depression large throngs of people parade along the front daily. (On) Sunday they were packed like sardines. The public houses are allowed to remain open until 11 o'clock at night. You have to go in the back streets to find them.'

NOW: Speedboat trips are still popular. A *007* boat departs from the end of the pier daily during the Easter holidays, then at weekends until Whitsun and daily from Whitsun until the end of September. Originally made of American mahogany and teak, and powered by ex-Navy S6 engines, the boats now have lightweight aluminium hulls and Roots Lister TS3 engines.

THE PIER EASTBOURNE. 8G.

THEN – EASTBOURNE PIER, *c*1904: An early view of the pier showing the original kiosks at the shore end. The pier was designed by Eugenius Birch and built at a cost of £13,300 from 1866. Lord Edward Cavendish opened the first section in June 1870. Work was completed in 1872, but the shoreward end was destroyed in a great storm in January 1877. The replaced section was built at a slightly higher level, and this discrepancy is still visible just north of the central pavilion.

PIER, EASTBOURNE.

FROM CHISLEHURST HOTEL.

THEN – EASTBOURNE PIER *c*1914: This later view of the pier shows alterations made to the entrance by the addition of a trio of picturesque kiosks. Note the rank of bath chairs on the right. These were a popular amenity in the early days of the century, and proprietors had their own association. In 1914 the charge for bath chairs was one shilling and sixpence for the first hour, and sixpence for each subsequent half hour.

51

Pier Entrance and Music Pavilion, Eastbourne

THEN – EASTBOURNE PIER *c***1929:** The Carpet Gardens are in the foreground and to the left the bath chairs stand in the rank. The pier is seen with the music pavilion, erected in 1924 at a cost of £15,000. Later the pavilion became a dance hall and, in 1968, an amusement hall.

NOW: Today the pier has yet another entrance. The original Victorian ticket kiosk was recently discovered in Gildredge Park where it had been used as a tool shed. The kiosk has now been restored by the Eastbourne Civic Society and in 1995 was set up outside the Redoubt Pavilion Tea Rooms where it is used as an ice cream kiosk and croquet set hiring point.The pier now has a pub and restaurant, a burger bar, family entertainment centres, various shops and a night club.

THEN – THE QUEEN'S HOTEL, SPLASH POINT *c*1905: The hotel was designed by Henry Currey and opened in June 1880. It was planned deliberately as a barrier dividing the high class hotels to the west from the boarding houses to the east. In 1722 the foundations of a Roman villa were found on its site, and during construction of the hotel two further discoveries were made.

NOW: Large quantities of shingle have changed the beach profile and a brick wall has been built between promenade and road. The exterior of the hotel has changed little over the years, except that two of the four rows of balconies have been removed. Also gone is the Eastern Bandstand, seen on the right of the old picture. In 1922 it was moved to the Redoubt Gardens.

Marine Parade Eastbourne.530.

THEN – PASSENGER SEAPLANE AND MARINE PARADE: An early seaplane is shown taking off from just east of the pier in about 1914. In 1921 Eastbourne Aviation Company ceased its joy rides from the beach after three crashes. In the background, from the left, are the Old Sea Houses, where Charles Darwin stayed while working on his book *Origin of Species*, the Albion Hotel and the Albemarle Hotel – originally the Anchor Inn, one of the earliest public houses in Eastbourne.

NOW: Little has changed, except that the Albion Hotel, now totally rebuilt internally, is called the Carlton Hotel. On the Albemarle, an anchor is still visible in the plasterwork on the exterior of the building just below the roof.

THEN – CAFFYN'S GARAGE: Caffyn's Garage was situated in Seaside Road, next to Marine Parade. On June 6, 1943, fourteen German Focke-Wulfe bombers made the last severe attack of the Second World War on Eastbourne and one of the 500kg bombs that fell destroyed Caffyn's. Nobody was hurt and staff were moved to the head office in Saffrons Road, except for the panel beaters and workers from the trimmers' paint shop, who were moved to other premises in Seaside. This postcard dates from 1907.

NOW: This island in the road was built on the site of Caffyn's Garage, and is situated at the junction of Marine Parade with Seaside and Seaside Road.

ROYAL PARADE, EASTBOURNE.

THEN – THE ROYAL MARINE HOTEL AND ROYAL PARADE, pu1923: The hotel, later renamed The Metropole, is on the left. It had a café on the ground floor open daily from 10.30am to 11pm. An open-top charabanc is parked in Royal Parade and a notice informs potential customers of the trips available.

NOW: On June 4, 1943, both the Metropole and the next door hotel, the Balmoral, since renamed the Glastonbury Hotel, were severely damaged by a 500kg enemy bomb. The Metropole has been rebuilt as the Metropole Court Flats. The photograph shows the brick wall that has been built between the promenade and the road, and the new high beach shingle.

THEN – ANGLES PRIVATE PENSION, ROYAL PARADE, pu1910: Here black and white minstrels can be seen playing outside the hotel; possibly they were members of Uncle Tom's Eastbourne Minstrels. A small boy is seen digging in the shingle at the top of the beach. Although bombs fell near the hotel during the Second World War, it remained open.

NOW: The balcony is still there today, but the Angles has been renamed the Majestic Hotel. The ground floor verandah has been enclosed to protect residents from the elements.

REDOUBT BANDSTAND, EASTBOURNE.

THEN – THE REDOUBT BANDSTAND: The Redoubt gardens and bandstand were directly to the west of the Redoubt fortress. The land was leased to Eastbourne Council in 1888 and a garden was laid out around the bandstand brought from opposite the Marine Gardens in 1922. The success of the Redoubt Music Gardens led to the provision of a stone-built bandstand and a partly covered auditorium where, up to the mid-1960s, all manner of entertainments took place, including Punch and Judy. This postcard dates from 1938.

NOW: The bandstand was demolished to make way for a sun lounge, although part of the auditorium remains. The sun lounge was built with money bequeathed by Harry Waghorn Ford, and was opened in April 1968. In 1994 the building was refurbished and became the Pavilion Tea Rooms. In 1995 the Victorian ticket kiosk from Eastbourne Pier was set up beside the tea rooms (see page 50).

Pevensey Bay 840

THEN – THE CRUMBLES *c*1910: This photograph was taken from Pevensey Bay looking back towards Langney Point and Eastbourne. The Crumbles was a bleak bank of windswept shingle. The only prominent buildings were the line of Martello towers. However, just prior to and during the First World War, it was the scene of much seaplane activity with the building and flying of aircraft from hangars on the shingle.

NOW: The area has been completely transformed by the Sovereign Harbour development, which consists of inner and outer harbours, shops, restaurants and 500 houses. Another 3,000 houses are planned, and a further harbour basin. When completed the development will almost link Eastbourne to Pevensey Bay. The building in the centre of this photograph is the Waterfront complex of restaurants, shops and offices.

THEN – WHITLEY ROAD BAND OF HOPE: Coal merchant Jack Hollands holds the horse's head as members of the Whitley Road Band of Hope prepare to leave on their Sunday School outing in 1909. In his book *Black Diamonds and White Cliffs,* Hollands states: 'It is certainly remembered that when the trade was at its slackest in the summer months the coal merchants could always be called upon to transport the children on their Sunday School outings'. The Band of Hope was a society promoting life-long abstention from alcohol for young people. It was founded in 1847.

NOW: Many of the buildings have changed little over the years. The Roman Catholic church of St Agnes, whose foundation stone was laid in 1906, is on the left. Then comes St Joseph's Catholic Centre, previously St Joseph's Catholic Schools, founded 1895. Next is St Agnes's Priests' House and, at the junction of Whitley Road and Seaside, just out of the picture, stands St Aidan's Methodist Church, whose foundation stone was laid in 1913.

THEN – WHITLEY ROAD AND BIRCHFIELD'S STORES 1940: On Sunday, July 7, 1940, a Dornier DO17 released a stick of ten high explosive bombs which fell on Whitley Road between St Philip's Avenue and Avondale Road. Two people died and twenty-two were injured. Nine houses were destroyed and six damaged. Two large gas mains in the road were fractured. Birchfield's Stores and sub post office at the junction of Clarence Road was destroyed, as was 38 Whitley Road.

NOW: The building that housed Birchfield's Stores was rebuilt and remained, until recently, the home of Miss Birchfield, daughter of the postmaster. In about 1952, 38 Whitley Road was also rebuilt and is now Junipers, a residential care home. On a telegraph pole in Clarence Road, a few yards from where the stores were, is the original sign now pointing to the new Whitley Road post office – now at 26 Stanley Road.

THEN – PEVENSEY ROAD: This 1905 postcard, illustrating the view down Pevensey Road from Susans Road, towards Seaside, shows small shops and a tea room on the left side of the road. On the right there were homes with just one shop, J H Dashwood and Son, furniture dealer, at number 15.

NOW: Visually, little has changed. On the left there are still shops with flats above. On the right there are residential properties with just one shop, Susan's Café, at the junction of Pevensey Road and Susans Road. The road is still tree-lined, but has now become a one-way street.

THEN – CHARLEY BROWN'S BARBER'S SHOP: Charley Brown 'hairdresser and perfumer' was to be found at 75 Susans Road, at the junction with Ashford Road. As well as haircutting, shaving and shampooing, Charley Brown stocked cigarettes and cigars. This postcard is dated 1908.

NOW: The shop front is little changed, but today Phantasia trades from number 75, selling board games, fantasy games, jigsaws and models.

The Princess Alice Memorial Hospital, Eastbourne.

THEN – THE PRINCESS ALICE HOSPITAL, CAREW ROAD: The hospital was built in memory of Princess Alice, Grand Duchess of Hesse, second daughter of Queen Victoria. She suffered from ill-health and convalesced in Eastbourne. She died in December 1878, aged thirty-five. On June 30, 1883, the Prince of Wales opened the hospital (and also the extended western promenade, the lawns on the sea front and the Bedfordwell pumping station). The postcard is dated 1913.

NOW: The hospital was demolished in 1998 and replaced by The Hawthorns, a retirement complex of 102 units catering for some 120 residents.

THE NEW POST OFFICE, EASTBOURNE. 540.

THEN – THE NEW POST OFFICE, UPPERTON ROAD *c*1915: The new post office, built on the old site of a large house called Yarra Yarra, is on the right in this view down Upperton Road towards Terminus Road and the railway station. The post office first appears in Gowland's Eastbourne Directory in 1915, before that Terminus Mansions was located in this area, also Eastbourne and District Motor Cab Company Limited.

NOW: The post office buildings have been enlarged and Upperton Road is now dual carriageway. Old Orchard Road and Grove Road are off to the right.

The Technical Institute, Eastbourne.

THEN – THE TECHNICAL INSTITUTE AND FREE LIBRARY, pu1907: In 1899 the eighth Duke of Devonshire donated a site in Grove Road for a public library and technical institute. The foundation stone was laid in 1903. The building, designed by P A Robson, cost £38,000. Andrew Carnegie donated £10,000 and the county council gave £2,000. The building was opened by the Duchess of Devonshire on August 8, 1904. It was destroyed by enemy bombing in 1943.

NOW: After being housed in temporary accommodation in Grand Parade, the new public library in Grove Road opened to the public on April 6, 1964. The photograph shows the new roundabout in Upperton Road. Old Orchard Road is on the right of the library and Grove Road to the left.

65 EASTBOURNE. — *Terminus Road.* — LL.

THEN – THE RAILWAY STATION *c*1905: Horse-drawn cabs wait for custom outside the station, the coal merchant's cart travels down the road and a telegram boy rides his bicycle towards the camera. Beyond the station is the Gildredge Hotel, which was badly damaged by enemy bombing on November 22, 1940. The original London Brighton and South Coast Railway line terminated at Polegate, but between 1846 and 1849 it was extended to Eastbourne and opened on May 14 when a special train ran from Brighton to Eastbourne.

NOW: The station has changed little, although the present building is the fourth on the site. This section of Terminus Road is now dual carriageway.

64 EASTBOURNE. — *Terminus Road.* — LL.

THEN – THE BRIGHTON ARMS, TERMINUS ROAD, *c*1905: This is the view down Terminus Road to the station. Cornfield Road is on the left and Junction Road on the right. The Brighton Arms at 59 Terminus Road was run by J Davies, wine and spirit merchant.

NOW: Today the view is very much changed. Parts of Terminus Road have become pedestrian precincts and the non-pedestrianised section is reserved for buses. Cornfield Road is still on the left but Junction Road has disappeared under the Arndale Centre, built in 1981.

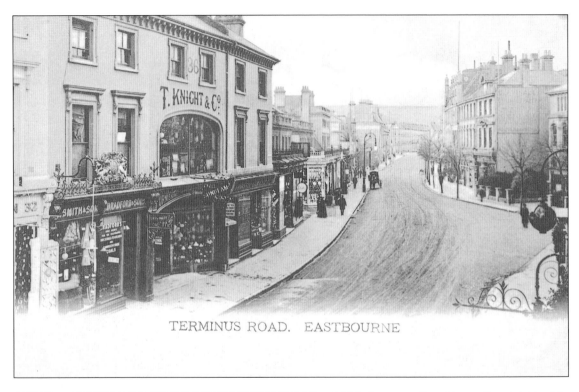

TERMINUS ROAD. EASTBOURNE

THEN – ANOTHER VIEW OF TERMINUS ROAD, *c*1904: Langney Road is on the right in this view down Terminus Road towards the station. On the left were an outfitter's shop, a coal and corn merchant, T Knight at 36, furnishing and general ironmongers, a wine, spirit and beer merchant, cycle agent and the General Post Office.

NOW: The same road is today a pedestrian precinct, with Debenhams occupying the place of the former small shops. Marks and Spencer, in the centre of the picture, occupies the site of Clement Vinall, general draper and house furnisher.

WAR MEMORIAL, EASTBOURNE.

THEN – THE WAR MEMORIAL, *c*1925: The memorial, which stands in Memorial Square, was built to commemorate the 1,056 men and women who were killed in the First World War. It was designed by Henry Fehr and unveiled by General Lord Horne on November 10, 1920. The square is at the junction of Cornfield Road, Bolton Road, Trinity Trees, Devonshire Place, Cornfield Terrace and South Street.

NOW: The memorial stands on a traffic island amid flower beds. Tablets inscribed to those who died in the Second World War have been added. The names of the dead of the 1939-45 war are on oak tablets in the Town Hall.

Eastbourne.   South Street and S. Saviour's Church.

THEN – SOUTH STREET AND ST SAVIOUR'S CHURCH: The viewpoint is from near where the War Memorial stands. The church was designed by G E Street and built in red brick. The almost freestanding tower was added in 1872. The delivery cart shown on page 3 belonged to high class grocer Cave, Austin & Co, at 110-114 South Street. The postcard is dated 1913.

NOW: The buildings on both sides of the street have changed little over the years although, of course, the shops are continually changing. The church is now St Saviour's and St Peter's, the latter named church in Meads Road having been demolished some years ago and replaced by flats.

THEN – ANOTHER VIEW OF SOUTH STREET, *c***1900:** The New Inn Hotel is seen on the right of this view from the Town Hall, looking down South Street. The tower of St Saviour's Church is clearly visible.

NOW: The road layout is very similar today. Buildings on the left side of the street include the Central Court (1879), The Masonic Hall and the South Street Free Church (1905). On the right the New Inn still stands, with its plaque dated 1880.

THEN – THE TOWN HALL: In 1852 the Vestry Room, forerunner of the present Town Hall, was built in Grove Road. In 1874 the Local Board, forerunner to the Town Council, proposed the building of a new Town Hall. It was designed in Renaissance style by W T Foulkes of Birmingham and the foundation stone was laid by Lord Edward Cavendish on October 9, 1884. It was built in dark red brick, dressed with Portland stone, on the site of the old Stocks Bank, previously the site of the St George's Day Fair (March 12) which was held up to the beginning of the 19th century. The Town Hall was completed in 1886 at a cost of £40,000. It was opened by the mayor, George Boulton, to the accompaniment of Handel's Hallelujah Chorus, Haydn's The Heavens are Telling and the National Anthem. The chiming clock for the 130ft high clock tower was added in 1892 at a cost of £700. When it first opened the Town Hall accommodated the corporation offices, the police and the county courts. This postcard is dated 1911.

NOW: The Town Hall building has changed little over the years, but the cottages on the left were replaced in 1910 by Caffyn's Garage and Saffrons Rooms. Caffyn's was founded by Percy Caffyn in 1902 and now has branches across the south east of England. His two sons, Edward and Sydney, both received knighthoods. Sir Sydney Caffyn was Mayor of Eastbourne from 1956 to 1958.

DALTON TERRACE MEADS, EASTBOURNE.

THEN – DALTON TERRACE, MEADS STREET: Looking down Meads Street, Dalton Road leads off to the right and Matlock Road joins from the left. The London and County Bank is in the centre of the photograph. The business in the centre of the terrace, the Meads Library, also published postcards of the area, including that featured on page 12.

NOW: The Meads branch of the National Westminster bank is on the corner where Dalton Road joins Meads Street. Dalton Terrace, with shops on the ground floor, and flats above, has changed little over the years.

Meads Street, Eastbourne, 441.

THEN – MEADS STREET: This postcard, which is dated 1907, features the bus used by the 'World's Oldest Municipal Omnibus Service', which was inaugurated on April 12, 1903. The service ran between Eastbourne Railway Station and Meads.

NOW: A modern bus is parked on almost exactly the same spot as its predecessor. A plaque on a house built in 1897, on the right hand side of the road, some fifty yards from the present Ship Inn, states that the premises are erected on the site of the Old Ship Inn which was built in about 1600. Meads Gate, a block of flats, has replaced the houses on the right of the postcard. The present Ship Inn replaces the old Ship Hotel.

GOLF LINKS, EASTBOURNE.

THEN – THE ROYAL EASTBOURNE GOLF CLUB, *c*1935: The Royal was founded in 1887 and over the decades has had a number of famous members, the earliest being H G Hutchinson, who won the Amateur Championship in 1886 and 1887, and in 1892 finished tenth in the Open at Muirfield, having led by three strokes after thirty-six holes. Ironically 1892 was the first year the Open Championship was extended from thirty-six to seventy-two holes. The Royal also boasts a Prime Minister among its former members – A J Balfour, who held office from 1902 to 1905.

NOW: The land on which the course is laid out is leased primarily from the Chatsworth estate and the Duke of Devonshire, who is the club's president; and a small part from the borough council. There are two distinctly named courses, the 18-hole Devonshire Course, par 71, and the Hartington Course of nine holes, par 32. On the left in the photograph is the Eastbourne College Astroturf which stands on land that until 1991 was part of Beresford House Girls' School. Next to the Astro is the site of the Eastbourne College Memorial Playing Fields. This was the home of St Cyprians', a boys' preparatory school that burned down during the night of Sunday, May 14, 1939.

THEN – SUMMERDOWN MILITARY CONVALESCENT CAMP, *c*1915: The camp was opened during the Great War, as a military convalescent hospital (1915-1920). It was in the area now occupied by Compton Drive, Old Camp Road and Pashley Road. In 1915 up to 3,500 troops, known as the 'Blue Boys' because of their distinctive uniform, were billeted in the camp. King George V and Queen Mary visited the camp. The building in the centre was, from 1939, the home of Beresford House School.

NOW: Today's view is taken looking down Compton Drive. Expensive houses have replaced the soldier's wooden huts. Beresford House School moved from The Avenue to new premises in Summerdown Road in 1939, and closed in December 1991. The main school building and gymnasium were demolished in 1995 and now the area is used for the Eastbourne College Astro, where games of hockey and tennis can be played in daylight or with the aid of floodlights.

THEN – ANOTHER VIEW OF SUMMERDOWN CAMP, *c*1915: Local photographers were kept busy during the whole period 1915-1920 taking views of the camp and of the men in their huts. This card shows the camp in the foreground with the newly constructed Compton Drive, Pashley and Uplands Roads behind. Numbers 67 and 69 Pashley Road are visible, as is the pavilion or clubhouse of the Eastbourne Downs Golf Links. The pavilion is now the Eastbourne Youth Hostel.

NOW: This photograph shows the Royal Eastbourne Golf Links in the foreground and to the left. Foredown Close and Fairway Close are in the right foreground, with Compton Drive, Old Camp Road, Pashley Road and Uplands Road towards the centre of the picture. The youth hostel is not now visible as the hillside is heavily wooded.

THEN – ST MARY'S CHURCH, OLD TOWN, *c*1910: Here, adjacent to the Lamb Inn, William Hurst founded the Star Brewery in 1777. On the left, opposite the Lamb, was the Manor House and gardens that belonged successively to the Gildredge and Gilbert families. In 1923 it was bought by the Eastbourne Borough Council and became the Towner Art Gallery. The church was built in the twelfth century to replace a Saxon church dedicated to St Michael, of which no trace remains.

NOW: The widening of the High Steet began after the First World War and led to what many consider to be the disfigurement of Old Town. In 1973 a shopping development was planned for the Star Brewery site and the interesting old building was demolished. Development was delayed and the Safeway store did not open until eleven years later. The Towner Art Gallery can be seen on the left of this photograph, and the Lamb Inn on the right.

CHURCH STREET

THEN – CHURCH STREET, OLD TOWN, *c*1915: Looking down Church Street, the Kings Royal Dairy is on the left and Vicarage Road and Brightland Road lead off to the right. The shops on the right included J W Walder, grocer, H Hudson, plumber, George Collins, bootmaker and Shadwell, builder. Then came the sub-post office, G H Chatfield and Son, dairyman, Griffin, confectioner, Ward butcher and Dann & Walder, fruiterers.

NOW: The scene is much changed. The shop on the left, Margaret Hunter, Ladieswear, in the premises of the old Kings Royal Dairy, closed some time ago and the building is now used as a carpentry store. The shops on the right have all been replaced with modern buildings.

THEN – THE LAMB INN, HIGH STREET, OLD TOWN, pu1910: The 14th century Lamb Inn, the oldest public house in Eastbourne, was built using local greensand. The postcard shows the unrecognisable exterior of the inn with its walls rendered with plaster. At the time the licensee was W F Walton who advertised for sale Bass's Pale and Burton Ales, Celebrated London Stout, Special Scotch and Irish Whiskies. There was also accommodation for cyclists and good stabling. In 1912 alterations were made to the inn and the plaster removed to reveal the original timbers.

NOW: The photograph shows the Lamb Inn on the left, and beyond it Safeway, which was opened by the mayor, Leslie Mason, on October 19, 1984. On the right, just below Borough Lane, is the Towner Art Gallery and Museum. Beyond the filling station on the right is the Prince Albert public house.

ABOUT THE AUTHORS

John Wilton was born in 1942 and educated at St Hugh's and St Edmund's College, Ware. After a short spell in the Army he entered teaching and since 1978 has run the Geography Department of St Andrew's School, Eastbourne.

He takes an active part in coaching sport, especially soccer, cricket and table tennis. His hobbies include photography, local history and long distance walking.

Chris Howden was born in London in 1938 and moved to Eastbourne in 1952. He was educated at Eastbourne College and has worked in the town since 1960, principally with the former Eastbourne Mutual Building Society. Between 1990 and 1998 he worked in the bursar's office at Eastbourne College.

His interests are walking, cycling, gardening and photography, combined with a keen interest in the town and surrounding villages.